SUNDIAL

poems by

Anika Jhalani

Finishing Line Press
Georgetown, Kentucky

SUNDIAL

Publisher: Leah Maines

Editor: Christen Kincaid

Author Photo: Sudhir Jhalani

Cover Design: Elizabeth Maines McCleavy

Printed in the USA on acid-free paper.
Order online: www.finishinglinepress.com
also available on amazon.com

Author inquiries and mail orders:
Finishing Line Press
P. O. Box 1626
Georgetown, Kentucky 40324
U. S. A.

I once met a boy who told me he wanted to be free. 💣

He told me smiling, arms folded behind his head. And the clouds floated up above him, silhouette and shadowing him, I traced the silver line of him into the sky. Holding on, I asked him. 'Free?'

And laughing, heartbreaking, he pushed me into the grass, took my collarbone between his teeth.

So I spread eye shadow like it's hope. Line these lids. Strut around in lamé silk outfits. Trying to keep him, keep this. I wrap myself in colors that shimmer under sun, hypnotize like panels of psychedelic fun, because you can't possibly want to be free of this, come on.

But in witnessing these attempts to keep him, he only laughed that terrible laugh again. Clasped the pearl of my earring between his teeth, pulled the adornments off me clean.

It's meaningless, he said. Be free.

Listen.

I've heard death comes in many forms, but my preferred are the boys. The kinds who sit on a sidewalk, absently flicking lighter without cigarette. The kinds who, if I asked them to, would pick me up effortless.

The kinds who can kill you, without even touching fist to flesh.

I'd had a couple of them before, those lovely massacres, those sweet ends.

The last one really stung, and I haven't played ever since.

But then there was this boy, another one, again.   💣

He came with a warning. 'I'll always be the one to leave. Someday this is going to end.'

But bubbling inside I rubbed the stubble on his jaw, traced the shape of his lips. Cotton candy, cola fizz, dissolving under my skin. Come on baby, leave? It's not gonna happen.

So we know the rules but choose not to play by them. Is it ignorance or innocence that gets us into trouble then?

Kids, just kids.

And then there was this boy, another one, again. 💣

Firecracker, a complete firework. Sparkling he'd set down his espresso, demand, 'tell me what you know.' He knew I knew him, knew him quicker than most, sometimes he liked this knowledge, sometimes it set off his temper. I'd pick up his cup he'd say 'no, no, no' because my lipstick got all over the rim, and he absolutely hated it, but I liked to light the wick to see his fire work.

I'll tell you what I know. I'll tell you something about yourself.

Gorgeous, absolutely mental. Total narcissist, but I'll feed your ego some more. Face evaded race, but you could place him from the middle of the world. Almond eyes, chin dimple. Looks can hurt.

He had these triceps, these arms full of flex and rest, sometimes he'd pick me up with them, say 'you know how in middle school they'd play a slow song for the slow dance,' I'd nod, 'that was my favorite part to ask a girl to dance' come here, and then I was in his arms my arms around his neck, lungs effervesced like champagne and, and…

Is it really true nothing lasts?

Girls adore him. He winks his four earrings catch the light in warning but the girls don't pay attention. Instead they reapply lipstick. I stand beside him. The beauties look me in the eye, for challenge or permission. I smile, 'go ahead.'

And here in the bar whose name is its number, the fizz of the beer, the rings in his ear, the atmosphere, it buzzes the girls senseless. They run palms up his arm hearts zip at his bicep. He crowns the barstool, I await the kill.

You really are beautiful.

He asks me if I'm a victim too, if I'm like the rest.
'Are you loving me now, do you want me now?'
I shake my head, I resist.

Billiard stick smacks into solid and striped pool balls. Red and yellow roll all over the table, but I only focus on the blue balls. Leaning over green velvet, I taunt boys he calls his friends. Gorillas scratch themselves. I gloss my lips.

The boys adore me as girls adore him, but when they ask for a kiss I never lean in.

Because while he wants liberation I seek something else. 💣

Splayed in bed I pull apart petals of flesh. Just beyond the window the sun's gone wild in her set. I locate the rose in my core to bloom it alive. The sun my witness, I open myself as she opens the sky.

The sun tears through the clouds with her box of watercolors. Autumn dusk chromes me. She dips into my bellybutton, brushes me flamingo pink. Smears blush over my body. Pours her gold into my pores, sparkles off my nails as they dig deep. I moan, but don't scream. I'm so beautiful, I'm so pretty. Flora and fauna coming with color, coming.

My body a tangerine. I peel skillfully. Pull apart each wedge, citrus bursts, streams down legs, I know how to do this. I know how to writhe. Touching myself beneath bed sheets I've practiced pretending to live.

Fruit and flowers open.
Almost there, I'm almost convinced.
But between a boy's touch and my own...
I can't deny the difference.

I called my ex-boyfriend, the first boy I loved.
'Do you think I'm resistible or irresistible?'
'Baby, not now.'
'Someday you're going to be my husband.'
'Rain check?' he said, and I laughed out loud. What's it been now? A year and a half?'
I hung up.

I called my second boyfriend, the one I'd loved but loved a little less.
The one who left me splintered, in a mess.
'Do you remember me?' I said.
Hadn't heard his voice in a year. And something that was once everything, he responded.
'Every little bit.'

I don't belong to anyone anymore, haven't belonged to anyone since.

Is this freedom? Is this what this is?

Listen.

I've heard boys come in many forms, but my preferred is death. Each time I kill myself for them, each time I love it. Pulled apart like an orange, I hand them each a fraction, to bite to pull off the rind, to consume so I can be kept.
All the clichés tell me, you can only die if you've lived.
So I take these beautiful boys, and turn them into death.

From my bed I slither to my vanity. Select a stick, scarlet lips. Mascara to lacquer lashes, I brush from base to tip. I admire myself. Am high on myself. I'm almost enough I'm almost convinced.

But when he calls me, I pick up.
'Donde?' he asks.
I think of his white teeth. I think of his smile on me.

You can only die if you've lived.

Come on, baby. At least I know the difference. ●⃰

We entered into a dance. He chose the music.

'All the girls fall in love with me. You won't, right? You promise?'

Before ten-ten. After eleven-twenty-five. Until seven. And then again at midnight. Spent swipes of lip gloss, missed assignments, the final weeks of college on him.

I'd be typing, writing away. Then I'd catch a flash of black, look up and those teeth that terrible bite of his, sinking into my shoulder blade, threatening to snap at my fingertip, 'come here,' he said, 'come on,' and then.

You made me laugh. When you pretended to fall, off your chair or in the library halls. Go ask for her number, I'd say, and he'd do it. He made fun of the acapella group, I muffled laughs into his armpit. Folded twenties into airplanes, flew them by the bill, missing it.

'Make your pecs dance.' Pop pop there they went.

His bite marks bruised my thighs. If you look close you can still see blue moons, blue crescents.

Reaching out, I traced the silver line of his lips.
Felt something beginning to take shape.

The way he saw the world. 'Sometimes I walk down the street pretending I'm retarded.' 'You can't be serious.' No I just want to be free of what other people think. Free of consequence, free of judgment. But I saw his world of so called freedom, and sometimes I didn't like it. Free or fear? I couldn't tell. 'Tell me about your ex-girlfriends,' I asked, and his arms alternated between flex and rest, between calm and tense, as he told me about her and her and another, his smile cracked like unwrapped secrets.

I fed. ✴

He chases girls, he spends himself within them. Clenches bird bones in his molar grip. They send him pictures of it afterwards, of the ways he blues and brands them, they ask for him again, but insatiable he finds another beauty at the bar and opens her up and empties himself.

He plays a mean game. He plays like a boy.

I watch him be free. I watch close.

But in the mornings he comes back to me. I make demands.
'Tell me I'm the most beautiful.'
'You're the most beautiful of them all.'
'Do you mean it?' I ask.
'No,' he says, and pulls my library chair closer to his, lips against my pulse.
'You're the moon and the sun.' ●※

But boys always go from gold to gone.

Kiss, it starts with a kiss. Then tongues feather to flames, they lick. Take advantage. Hickey me to heat. Suck me. Vermillion. Eat me white hot. Blaze me bronze, brazen. I'll be burned be bruised, beg but be refused, I know how it'll go, we'll be dancing in your room, and then without warning, without relenting, time will set fire to you.

We sway through the smoke. Ocher I ache, knowing you'll disappear. Singed you'll lead my palm to grip your finger, spinning us you'll sear but slow, I want a slow burn. Please don't go, I want another turn.
And just when I think time might stop.
Like summer you'll have simmered from gold to gone.

Boys like you, they remind me of the rules. Those hands that match, tick, tick. Fingers teasing lighters, no more cigarettes. Nothing lasts, it can't. Unless.

If we can't break the rules, could we at least bend them?
Tick, tick, trick.

Could you stay for just a minute? Listen. 💣

I once met a boy who wanted to be free.

He told me humming as he fractioned a peach. Ticking me off, I reached to still his hand. Traced veins from elbow to wrist. Pulled underneath his bracelet, a scar knifed thick under black thread. Free, I said.

And biting, smiling, he split the fruit, fed me the last piece.

Sunlight yellowed him as he made towers with our books. I liked to look. How nectarined fingers stacked o-chem for the base, balanced novellas on top, I helped him build up. He peeked at me behind peached pages. Shy, I laughed, 'stop.' Slice. Ouch. Papercut. Reaching for my wrist, he took my thumb to his lip. Watching me watch him he tongued the blood.
'Hey,' I scolded.
'What?'
And under the steam of the espresso machine, between lattes and buttery things, winter mornings we were supposed to study, he gave me himself. Pulled his past apart, slices of citrus I sucked. Sour. Puckered. Ouch. Because when I asked him, 'haven't you ever been in love?' he only shrugged and said, 'enough is always enough.'

And then I couldn't help myself.

Apricots of aphrodisiac bore about my skin. Whetted I craved the kill, ripe for his bite. I wanted him. Complicit he ran his palms over the book spines. Pages smooth as flesh, biology and logic trembled under his grip. Selecting a textbook he held the skeleton above him, teasing me, knowing me, he pulled it open.
'It's all here,' he warned me. 'Everything ends.'

Maybe the things you read shape your beliefs. Maybe I could change that.

I wish I could be beautiful enough.

'Maybe get your hands on some fiction.'

So in a café, in the library, or folded on his black sheeted bed.
A sunburst contracted his pupils, starry eyed he leaned in.
As he smoothed out my creases, as he underlined my skin.

I wrote myself into something that could keep him.

And he read. 💣

I pretend.

Nights the moon bathes me with herself, orbits as I undo myself with thumbs full of you, attempts at your touch. Blisters, rub, not enough. What would it be to love? On. You.

Give me something, a silver sliver.
Come here. Come on. Don't be a cloud.

Nights I lie in bed alone, the moon winks in crescents, coquettish. She's in circles for someone too, she knows. So she aids me as I'm lying. Pale she pours. As we pretend it's not my body doing the work, but yours.

You're reeling me in with the line, getting me high.
I cull memories, twist them to my hopes.

Him and his roommate in bed. I climbed in with them. Israeli accents, 'lamb has come to lions' den.' He pulled off my socks, brushed mouth against bare tendons. I peeked under the covers. Both boys had boxer tents. Did they or didn't they? I was shy. Fizzing, bubbling. Those almond eyes. Heat spilled. Take us out of the almost. I want to be killed.

By your mouth.
Your tongue is a match of mine. Got a light?
I can make you char like time.

But it's night and only the moon tumbles into my hair, strokes my body, it should be you not her nor me. I taste bitter blood as I bite, it should be you paper cutting, your celestial teeth.

Bracelets become handcuffs. Choker chokes my neck.
Stars like bars wrap my body when…

At night I write about a boy.

And open. 💣

Could art change your mind, could it change fate?
Could I make myself worthy of your taste?
Spring came.

I broke in new sandals, blisters bubbled about my ankles. I slathered honey across my peach fuzz, the wax bore me a smooth gold. Sacrificing skin, I edited flesh and page. I wrote.
He read.
Summer marbled me sunburnt and tan. Pendants of sweat nectared my neck. He lapped up the jewels. Gorged on gorgeous fruit. Bit to the pit, then spit.

Girls glistened in the distance, witnessed.
Desiring me, discarding me, he lured them in.

Plucking me beneath the cherry trees, he peeled me out of clothes. Licked me electric. Nibbled my nipples. I pushed him off, 'don't use me,' don't whore me to get girls. He wiped his mouth, 'just help me out,' unraveling my body he took his fill.

Girls glistened in the distance, impressed.
I really am beautiful.

So he spent my beauty on himself. Dozens of ditzes thirsty for indiscretion, spying they'd stiletto close, close. Beckoning, he tucked thumbs under thong straps. Snapped.
'Isn't she your girlfriend?' they giggled.
He pinched my ass. 'Almost.'

Sweat collected behind my knees. Heat pooled in my collarbone. He liked me like that, dripping. Splashed me wet, with jealousy. Lip cuffing ear lobes, edging blondes into bar corners. I called, 'come back,' he shimmered, 'later, later.'
Hands ticking, lower, lower.

I pulled him back, we danced. Unbuttoning his shirt, I made my demands.

'Tell me I'm the prettiest.'
'You're old news.'
'You said I was the moon.'
'No one at this school is going to remember you,' he said.
'As long as you don't forget.'

Dandelions break below breath. Eyelashes like doves, wished upon, sent.

Ok, ok. It's time now. 💣✳

If you're a boy, be death.

Remember, a year ago, the day we met?
You could have been.
Just someone reading on the steps.

But these organs knew better. The body cannot be tricked.
Heart broke in piñata, confetti dizzied my belly. Who is this snack? He
licked to turn the page, shadows slit his wrists. Dimples, those dimples.
Mirage or miracle?

I didn't know you then.

Closing in, I twisted see what you read. Cirrus feathered
campus, laughter tickled the air. You underlined a page, pencil bobbing
in your mouth. Chewed lead like it was licorice. Yuck. Innocent to what
lay ahead, but complicit nonetheless. I willed you, sun struck.

Look up.

What's going to happen now?

Someday we'll be formal with each other. I'll ask how medical
school's going, you'll be too polite to tell me I have lipstick on my teeth.
We'll pretend you weren't a paradise a parasite, that you didn't make
me bloom and bleed. Your sandalwood skin will only be the shell of a
past.

It's true that nothing lasts.

Once I didn't know you'd be a sundial to me.

Drowsy he doused himself in summer's last drops. Dots
formed ellipses for a story yet to come.

We think we get to decide.
We think we write.

He looked up. I smiled.
Winked.

Ori, come on. We were never free. 💣

Sunday before his birthday, up to his apartment 4B. I wrapped my wrists, a noose around his neck. Shrugging loose, 'let's just go,' he said.

It could have been, it could have been.

We zigzagged campus, we zigzagged through the park. He tugged on my blue silk dress. Embroidery crumpled in his palms. He sprayed me with water. Carried me over a fence. Placed his mouth on my forehead, retracted, second-guessed. 'What's wrong,' I said.

'If you ask me that again I'm going to leave. Actually I do want to leave.' Downtown by now, I tiptoed to near his mouth, sucked. Left behind a crescent of cinnamon gum. 'It's you,' I said, 'I want you so much.'

'Enough,' he said. 'Stop it. Enough.'

He made a face, erased my kiss from his cheek. But the boys become everything to me. I unzipped his jacket, his shadow fell fleeting on the currents in the river, like fizz again he slipped through my fingers, my braceleted fist, his constant resist, the lust of sudden dusks, consuming, relentless.

Have we never been here, or have we been here a thousand times before?

And endless, dazzling fractal, will we only repeat ourselves?

Don't make me live forever. 💣

It had to stop. I ran to the shop. And the cashier blew up the birthday balloons, some metallic some patterned I picked one in each color only repeated the reds. 'Fill them up, all twenty-five of them!' I said, and those balloons filled with more than helium.

Dreams tucked beneath the latex.

Because it happened just as I knew it would. 'I don't want to see you again,' he said.

'Don't do this,' I said, tracing the apple on his throat, cherries of his lips. He swallowed, a shadow. I winced.

'I told you I would leave,' he smiled. 'You chose not to listen.'

But can't you be convinced? 💣

Eclipse. Twins of time, mouths full of each other, kiss.

Moon-dusted. Glittering under the bronze border of the sun.
I wrote about someone.

Maybe I can't break you, but I can make you bend.

Sometimes the moon and sun eclipse. Sometimes, time stalls.
Look, I've thought about it.

Writing about you is not so different. I can stop time, relive, relive,
relive it.

Are you reading this right now?

Solitary, solar, lunar, lunatic.
Playing on sheets, I make the impossible happen.

What if I wrote this beautifully enough?

Comma, comma, comma.
I touch myself, I touch myself.

Could art turn time around?
Could art make you return?

Moon on sun.

Your gaze on this page means you're here with me now.

Come. ☄

The shopkeeper called, 'your order is ready for pick up,' but I didn't go. Days did their damage on balloons, but I let them deflate, I wrote.

Tomorrow was my deadline to finish. Then I wanted to make it better so I blazed through two more weeks, then three. Scalding skies, devouring nights, fractioning afternoons. Writing. Days lengthening, graphite sharpening, we were no longer speaking. Racing to get time back. Summer simmering we only had one week left...

Balloons or bombs, balloons or bombs?
A wish packed beneath each sentence.

Bottles of champagne popped open, diamonds clattered into crystal glasses. Bubbly families guzzled the gems. Square hats tossed into creamsicle sunsets, tassels striped the melting wind. Graduation came and went. But I hadn't finished, hadn't tricked us back. And I knew no matter what I did...

We'll never be kids again.

Packed my dorm into cardboard boxes. Removed paperbacks from their shelves.
Edged my way into the park, alone.
Balloons or bombs. I let them go.
Color sparkled in the sky.
Skimmed the clouds, the silver lines.
It could have been a concession, a goodbye.
But then I reconsidered.

Because if you're made of freedom, I am of hope. 💣

I know a boy who wants to be free.

He tells me winking, arms folded behind his head. And the clouds blot him out, as do the moon and the sun, time chars him the days drop three, two, one. Dawn you'll be gone. 'Holding on,' I ask you, 'free?'

And laughing, heartbreaking, he crumbles me between his teeth.

So I rush these words. Type these sentences. Adorn so you'll adore. I want to keep you, keep this. I honeycomb through details, resurrect the fun, because if you're reminded too you can't possibly leave me like this, come on.

But I can't be sated staying in sheets alone.
Time ashes relentless, but look, we've still got a minute.

Ori, listen.

Boys came in many shapes, but the best brought shade. Sunsets they crushed me hushed me, cremated with teeth and threats. Smoked me slowly, like the final cigarette.
They weren't confined to dreams. I know you exist.

I play on the page because I'm afraid, but it's no life without death.
You're free to decide. But I won't write goodbye.

If only tonight, if just for tonight.   💣

I hope we live our end. 💣💣💣

Anika Jhalani lives and writes in Coney Island, New York. She previously worked for Scholastic, the children's book publisher, and is a graduate of Columbia University, where she studied creative writing and business management. Her fiction and essays have been published in *StoryQuarterly, Cathexis Northwest Press, Whiskey Island*, among other publications.